THOU WHEN THOU PRAYEST

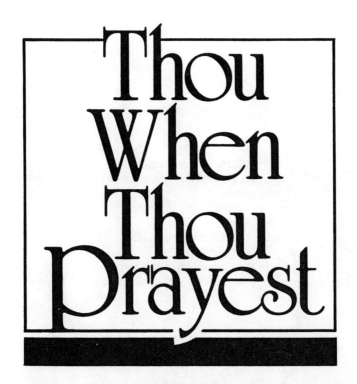

Thou When Thou Prayest

William Owen Carver

BROADMAN PRESS
Nashville, Tennessee

© Copyright 1987 • Broadman Press
© Copyright 1928 • The Baptist Sunday School Board
All rights reserved
4269-46
ISBN: 0-8054-6946-X
Dewey Decimal Classification: 248.3
Subject heading: PRAYER
Printed in the United States of America
Library of Congress Catalog Card Number: 87-15066

Library of Congress Cataloging-in-Publication Data

Carver, William Owen, 1868-1954.
  Thou when thou prayest.

  Reprint. Originally published: Garden City, N.Y.:
Doubleday, Doran, 1928.
  1. Prayer.   2. Lord's prayer.   I. Title.
BV210.C35   1987   248.3'2   87-15066
ISBN 0-8054-6946-X

TO
OTHERS WHO SEEK
THE FATHER'S FACE

CONTENTS

PUBLISHER'S INTRODUCTION

Thou When Thou Prayest was first published in 1928. Since that time, many helpful books on prayer have been released—some of them by Broadman Press. Why then should Broadman reissue a book that is sixty years old when so many useful, more recent ones are available? We want readers to know the why and how for publishing this volume in 1987.

The author of *Thou When Thou Prayest* was William Owen Carver. This fact in and of itself is reason enough for many people. W. O. Carver was a remarkable, influential man. The second of eleven children, he was born April 10, 1868, in Wilson County, Tennessee. Interestingly enough, the struggling Southern Baptist Theological Seminary was only nine years old when Carver was born. He later spent more than sixty years of his life related to this institution. His name is still mentioned in the classrooms and halls of this seminary. Carver died in Louisville, Kentucky on May 24, 1954. What manner of man was he?

Carver received the M.A. degree from Richmond College in Richmond, Virginia in 1891. Prior to going away to college, he told his mother, a devout Christian who was a strong influence in his life, he felt called to the ministry. During his years in Richmond, Carver had his first experience serving as a pastor. After college, he became pastor of his home church where he was ordained on December 25, 1891.

Carver began his studies at Southern Seminary in 1891. He left the seminary in 1893 and became professor of philosophy and ancient languages in Boscobel College in Nashville, Tennessee. He also served as pastor of South Union Church in Church Hill, Kentucky. Carver returned to Southern Seminary in January 1895 and received the Th.M. degree that year. He received the Th.D. degree in 1896.

Carver was something of a pioneer among Southern Baptists in the areas of missions and comparative religion. He began his teaching career at Southern Seminary as an instructor in New Testament in 1896. He also taught some in the fields of homiletics and theology. Carver introduced a course in comparative religion and missions in 1899, and the direction of his teaching career was set. He became head of the missions department in 1900 and served in that position until his retirement in 1943.

At a time when Southern Baptists faced theological problems early in this century, Carver sought to stretch the denomination beyond sectarian isolation. Through his writings, teaching, and personal ministry, he called for a fresh understanding of Paul's concept of the church, especially as expounded in Ephesians. The results of his years of study and involvement in this pursuit were published in *The Glory of God in the Christian Calling* (1932).

Carver's personal service matched his teaching in the classroom. He represented the seminary as a member of the executive committee of the American Association of Theological Schools from 1936 to 1944. He was a member of the American Theological Committee, a subsidiary of the World Conference on Faith and Order—from its beginning in 1939. Carver was a key figure in the founding of the Woman's Missionary Union Training School at Southern Seminary in 1907. He taught there while also teaching at the seminary. In 1953 the name of the school was changed to The Carver School of Missions and Social Work.

An interest in missions was accompanied by an interest in history. Carver was a charter member and for a long time was president of the Southern Baptist Historical Society. He was largely responsible for founding the Historical Commission of the Southern Baptist Convention. A room in the Historical Commission offices continues to honor William Owen Carver.

Carver's writing ministry was impressive. He was the author of nineteen published books, managing editor of the *Review and Expositor* from 1920 to 1942, contributing editor of the *Commission* for twelve years, and a frequent contributor to journals.

Readers will discover that *Thou When Thou*

Prayest is much more than an old book. Some pages will be very contemporary. Carver deals, for example, with the plight of the poor, homeless, and hungry and with some of the concerns of Bible study and exegesis. Indeed, readers are urged to read this volume with a Bible close by. You will need to review a number of Bible passages to receive the richness this slender volume has to offer.

No one currently working with Broadman Press knew W. O. Carver. Some have read his books—both as textbooks and as significant leisure reading. Others have heard professors refer to Carver as the white haired gentleman who walked the campus and continued to work with and influence students through the years of his retirement. He is remembered as being tough, fair, sometimes argumentative, and above all a Christian with a deep concern for the course of Christian missions—around the world and through churches as Christians share the message of the good news of Jesus Christ.

What manner of man was Carver? A man of influence and importance for those interested in Baptist history and heritage and who search for models of scholarship and leadership. His shadow reaches into the present generation, and we at Broadman Press believe that we still can learn from this man through his life and thought.

Preparing this material for republication was an interesting journey for Broadman personnel, and we want readers to know what decisions were made during this time. Our first inclination was to treat the book copy as we would any other manuscript in the editorial process. Numerous changes were made in style, word usage, and punctuation. In a few places questions were asked about the appropriateness of preserving statements that might not be as relevant in 1987 as they were in 1928. However, the more this kind of work was done, the more it was obvious that we were losing Carver—the man and the circumstances in which he wrote this fine book. Consequently, the decision was made to leave the material as it was first published in 1928. A few typographical errors were corrected during the typesetting process. What you have in hand, then, is a 1928 book by William Owen Carver in contemporary typesetting and binding.

Here are some of the items you need to know as you study this book. Carver apparently assumed that readers would use his book with Bibles in hand. Hence he did not identify the source of each verse quoted. Current style requires careful identification of each reference. We decided to leave the material as first written. Sometimes Carver used quotation marks when he obviously was summarizing a Scripture passage. In this reissued volume, we left this form intact in most places. Several stylistic changes would be necessary to give this book a "1987 flavor." We now capitalize words that Carver did not; punctuation does not always agree with current usage in Broadman books; and some of his phrasing sounds very much like 1928.

Furthermore, Carver made no effort to indicate which translation of the Bible he used—as would be expected today. Some of his references seem to be from the King James Version; others seem to be the American Standard Version; most appear to be his own translation. Carver was competent in Greek and often made his own translations. We did not try to identify versions but to leave Carver's material as presented in its original form. You will be able to make your own comparisons as you study.

These items are indicated so you will be aware

of the vintage of this book. We simply want readers to know that the decision to "leave Carver as Carver" was made intentionally. We are aware that this volume does not always match current writing style, but it does preserve a glimpse of our heritage through W. O. Carver.

Broadman Press is pleased to make *Thou When Thou Prayest* available once again. Now that you know a little bit about Carver and the editorial/production process, with Bible in hand you are ready for the pages that follow. We trust and pray that this book will be useful to you and offer suggestions that will become partial answers to the request of the disciples that also is ours: "Lord, teach us to pray."

Much of the information on Carver's life is from *Encyclopedia of Southern Baptists* (Nashville: Broadman Press, 1958), I, 236.

I

THE BACKGROUND

I

THE BACKGROUND

Jesus was the *Supreme Man of Prayer*. Nothing is more characteristic of him. Nothing more arresting. He lived by prayer. He met all his crises in prayer. The Gospel accounts of his birth and childhood reflect an environment and an atmosphere of reverence, worship, prayer. Our first view of him is in the temple, his Father's "house of prayer for all nations." At his baptism he prayed and the heavens were opened for the voice of approval and for the descent of the Holy Spirit to abide upon him. In the wilderness experience when he faced the definition of the principles on which he would undertake and carry through his life mission, and in which he resisted "every temptation" of the Devil, "He fasted forty days"—always a special preparation and experience of prayer—; and when the Devil had left him, angels ministered unto him and "he returned in the power of the Spirit into Galilee" (Lu. 4:1-14).

It was "as he was praying apart" and his disciples were with him that he drew from them the confession of Peter of his divine Sonship and Messiahship. This was followed by a severe crisis with the twelve over the question of his death which he was now beginning to teach must be experienced in Jerusalem, a year prior to the event; and when it looked as if a breach was imminent between them and him, Jesus chose three of them to go with him "into the mountain to pray. And as he was praying, the fashion of his countenance was altered, and his raiment became white and dazzling." "And behold, there talked with him two men, who were Moses and Elijah; who appeared in glory, and spoke with him about his decease which he was about to accomplish at Jerusalem. And a voice came out of the cloud, saying, This is my Son, my chosen: hear ye him" (Lu. 9:18-36; Mt. 16:13-17; 8).

When Jesus had gained a wide popularity, was

followed by multitudes of more or less sincere believers, and the time had come for him to effect a simple organization of his helpers and begin the organization of his permanent institution, he spent an entire night alone in prayer, considering and conferring in spiritual fellowship with his Father the names of men whom he might make into apostles. In the morning he came down from the mountain with his list in mind and "called his disciples; and he chose from them twelve, whom also he named apostles" (Lu. 6:12-19). When the first great wave of superficial popularity swept upon him by reason of his healing the sicknesses of the people, "he arose a great while before day and went out into a desert place, and there prayed," thus determining upon the course that led him away from crowded Capernaum on "into the next towns" (Mk. 1:35-39).

The last year of his ministry is one of intense situations, deepening conflicts, of what would be constant, exhausting strain but for some extraordinary upbearing within the soul of Jesus. And the spirit of prayer marks the year all the way through. The consciousness of dependence on his Father and of the answering oneness with

the Father impress one more and more. It was in
this period that we find the Twelve most impressed by this prayerful attitude, although they
were puzzled by it and sought in vain to compre-
hend his praying.

When he was called to the death-bed of Laza-
rus and came only for the after-burial mourning
his most amazing miracle was commanded in
the midst of praiseful prayer.

When Greeks came seeking to meet Jesus at
the very close of his ministry in the temple, he
seemed to be transported by the fact and in spirit
inquired how he should meet his crisis of being
"lifted up." The answer he found in a prayer that
the Father would glorify his own name in the sac-
rifice. The Father's answer came with strong assurance and his satisfied soul proclaimed: "I, if I
be lifted up from the earth will draw all men unto
myself" (Jno. 12). Thus for the third time God
bore audible witness to his Son, and approval of
him; and every time the witness came as he was
in prayer.

The upper-room conference with the Twelve
(Jno. 13—16) is the Holy of holies of the association of this group of men; and who can read the

record without the deepest sense of worshipful reverence. It is in effect a prolonged prayer. The evening closes in the most remarkable prayer of his life of prayer, that of the seventeenth chapter of John, wherein his work, his spiritual children, the whole lost world press hard upon his heart and are lifted up to his Father.

From this prayer he goes into Gethsemane and in an agony of soul beyond our comprehension won his supreme victory and came forth to accept all the shame of crucifixion.

He was nailed to the cross in prayer, in prayer marked the stages of his dying and in prayer breathed out his spirit into the Father's security. Can we think it strange, then, that at the Ascension day it is not in prayer but in the blessing of One to whom henceforth men may pray and will pray that he appears and disappears in a cloud that received him out of physical sight? His life of prayer has brought his followers into such a relation to him that they can return from Olivet "to Jerusalem with great joy; and were continually in the temple blessing God."

Jesus is *the supreme Teacher of Prayer*. To be sure his example was Jesus' greatest lesson in prayer.

The only record of his disciples asking that he would teach them to pray was called out by his praying. "And it came to pass, as he was praying in a certain place, that when he closed, one of his disciples said unto him, Lord, teach us to pray" (Lu. 11:1). It was not this prayer alone that caused the request to be made at this time. The occasion was late in his ministry, and indicates that his prayer life had so deeply impressed them by this time that they had come to feel that he knew prayer as they did not, and as they had never before witnessed prayer in the life of a man. They had come to connect his extraordinary powers, his superman insight, his transcendent character and his moral mastery of men, including themselves, with his unmatched communion with his Father.

There is no account of any formal discourse on prayer by the Lord. There are many instances of teaching prayer in the midst of other teachings, or brief exhortations and instructions concerning this great experience.

"He spake a parable unto them that to this end, that men ought always to pray and not to faint" (Lu. 18:1). This parable of the "importunate widow" was matched in teaching by that of the friend seeking the loaves at midnight (Lu. 11:5-13). In both Jesus strongly urged that the heavenly Father stands eagerly ready to give to them who come to him; but that he is hindered in giving his best gifts by the lack of earnestness and of faith on the part of the petitioners. Isn't that the meaning of the question (Lu. 18:8): "Nevertheless, when the Son of man cometh, shall he find faith on the earth"? He comes to bring the answer of the Father in blessing; but finds no receiving faith, and is unable to deliver the good things which the Father would so freely give.

Mountains may be moved, even as, and as easily as, the fig tree was withered if only there be unwavering faith; "if the man who prays shall not doubt in his heart, but shall believe that that which he saith cometh to pass; he shall have it." The Master continues: "Therefore I say unto you, all things whatsoever ye pray for, believe that ye receive them and they shall be given you" (Mk. 11:20-26).

Thus Jesus teaches that prayer is both a great privilege and a supreme duty. It is the experience by which we come into such relation of unity and cooperation with God that all things become possible to our faith. See, for examples, Mt. 18:18-20; Jno. 14:13; 15:7, 16, 23; 16:23-24.

Jesus taught that he depends for the success of his work on the capacity of his followers in prayer and their faithfulness in praying. See John 15:16; Mt. 18:18-20. "In his name" and as his representatives they (we) are to carry on in his work and his kingdom, and in that responsibility we are to have unlimited access to the resources of heaven which the Father will open for us when we pray.

A remarkably significant teaching of Jesus about prayer—set down by Matthew as a part of the Sermon on the Mount (7:7-12)—indicates that the way to generous right-living in our social relations is to be sought and found only in such a praying relation to God as brings us to "ask," "knock" and "seek" at heaven's gate so effectively that unlimited stores are available unto us. "Therefore" and thus alone, can we adopt the Golden Rule as our standard in social contacts.

Jesus pledges himself perpetually to pray for us if, and as, we represent him and go on to do his "greater works." See John 14:16. And yet we must not be misled by this promise, "for the Father himself loveth you, because you have loved me, and have believed that I came forth from the Father" (Jno. 16:27). This dependence of Jesus on praying, believing, working followers, is in harmony with the call of Ps. 72:15, where it is said of the Messianic King that "men shall pray for him continually."

Born into a circle so manifestly given to prayer, Jesus grew into a man of prayer. Bearing a burden such as never fell upon human heart he was driven to "offer up prayers and supplication with strong crying and tears unto him that was able to save him from death, and having been heard for his godly fear, though he was a Son, yet learned he obedience by the things which he suffered; and having been made perfect, he became unto all them that obey him the author of eternal salvation; named of God a high priest after the order of Melchizedek" (Heb. 5:2-10).

It is this Jesus who teaches us "The Lord's Prayer" which we undertake to study here, once again.

Its setting in the Sermon on the Mount is instructive. Luke reports it in still briefer form as given much later and in response to a request of the disciples that he teach them to pray (11:1 ff.). If we assume that both Matthew and Luke report correctly the circumstance of the teaching, then it is quite natural that Luke's version should be shorter; for, in that case, the Lord would merely remind them that he had already given them the lesson. Only they had not learned it, in its deeper meaning. It was not a new prayer they needed but new insight, deeper earnestness, more devotion, a more vital faith, a more forgiving spirit, so that they might truly, honestly, genuinely pray as already he had taught them.

In Matthew the Prayer is set in the heart of the Sermon in which Jesus sets forth his ideals for the men of his kingdom. The occasion was the pressure of the multitudes that were coming to Jesus from all sections of Palestine. The time had come for beginning the organization of his work and his workers. Having chosen the Twelve (Cf. Lu. 6:12 ff.), he addressed his disciples, including especially these newly appointed helpers who were henceforth to be continuously associated with him and to share his work and plans.

As Matthew (Chs. 5—7) preserves the outline

for us Jesus begins with setting forth the qualities of men who belong to the kingdom of heaven, qualities that mark men as "blessed" (5:3-10).

Then he brings out the functions of those who are his followers—members of his kingdom. They are "prophets," who speak in behalf of him; "salt," through which God saves his world; "light," by which men are led to glorify the Father in heaven. (5:11-13).

Next Jesus states, with amplification and illustrative examples, the moral and ethical standard for members of the kingdom of heaven. They are to be perfect even as their Father in heaven is perfect (5:17-48).

Thus he leads up to the paragraph containing the teaching as to prayer. (6:1-18). The topic of the paragraph is *Honesty in our Acts of Worship to God*. He selects for emphasizing this demand of honesty in worship the three most characteristic of Jewish forms of religion: almsgiving, prayer, fasting. He takes them in that order. The opening exhortation applies to all three: "Take heed that ye do not your righteousness before men to be seen of them: else ye have no reward with your Father who is in heaven." Whatever we do in

worship, as a part of our religion, as an expression of our righteousness, must be done definitely, exclusively toward God, for his eye alone.
If we do it to be seen of men we have gotten
thereby all that is to be gained by us. It ceases to
be religious, worshipful or righteous, and becomes only an ostentatious self-exploitation. It
was done "to be seen of men." Men have seen.
"You have received-in-full your reward."

II

APPROACH

II

APPROACH

Jesus leads cautiously into the presence of God. Let there be no impetuous rush at the throne, no thoughtless and irreverent demanding of things, no self-important and self-assuming boldness. A man in need is approaching the God of the universe. There must be preparation for prayer. The self needs searching preparation and the prayer needs reflection, meditation, ordering. Both in private and in public prayer there is far too much of the impulsive, and impromptu, the merely emotional. Jesus bids us pause and prepare as we approach.

Two dangers he warns us against.

First, there is the arrogance of the Pharisee;

next, the ignorance of the heathen. Both are fatal to true prayer. "When ye pray, ye shall not be as the hypocrites." They mask their real motives. They often deceive themselves. They seek to deceive others. "They love to stand and pray in the synagogues and in the corners of the streets, that they may be seen of men." There is the deceit and the hypocrisy. The Greek text emphasizes the deliberate seeking of attention and public notice. "They love to pray after having taken up a position," and "in order that they may be manifest to men."

The parable of the Pharisee and the Publican was addressed to "certain who trusted in themselves that they were righteous and set all others at naught" (Lu. 18:9 ff.). "The Pharisee, when he had taken his stand, addressed these (words) unto himself in prayer." Jesus did not admit that this was any prayer unto God. In form the man addressed God; in fact he was but talking to himself. He did not have his mind upon God nor his eyes toward heaven. His eyes were not shut for meditation. He saw the publican and he thought of men. "God, I thank thee that I am not as the rest of men . . . even as this publican." He thought of other men and of their sins—not to grieve over their sins, nor to seek their rescue. There was no plea for pity, no longing that they might be better. Rather was there the pride of superiority. God is invited to look upon the righteousness of the man who stands before him.

He saw the publican, although the publican "stood afar off" by the door of the synagogue, feeling himself unfit even to approach the prayer place, but driven thus far by his sense of great need and unfitness, while the Pharisee was standing at the front. He saw him, saw only what the poor man was in his social position, but not at all who he was in his self-loathing and heart-longing. The poor sinner was so sincerely penitent and so longing for mercy that he admitted the truth of all that was implied in the Pharisee's taunt—for the form of statement suggests that the Pharisee spoke so as to cause the publican to hear. He smote his breast, saying, "God be merciful to me the sinner." "The" sinner probably means "the one singled out in the prayer of the Pharisee."

The picture of the parable is, of course, a cartoon; but like all good cartoons it emphasizes the actuality. There is real danger that we shall be self-righteous, hypocritical, contemptuous, eager for credit from men; and all this in our very acts of religion. Jesus knew our human nature when he warned us to take pains to be honest with God. Of all places to strut, prayer would seem to be the last. Yet pride in prayer is more than possible. There is no danger more subtle than to win a reputation for fluency, eloquence, power in prayer. The danger reaches its worst when one is praised—or even thanked—for the qualities of humility, reality, spiritual grip in his public prayers. And what of the man who will not pray in public because he is not fluent, or eloquent, or "gifted"? Is it not pride of human judgment that deters him? That is a great story of Stonewall Jackson who insisted, when convinced that it was his duty, that he be called on to pray even though he made a pitiable mess out of it, and persisted until he became a man of might in prayer, and left an influence for godliness that abides.

There are two aspects of the hypocrisy in prayer: the eye for honor from men, and the conceit of personal worth. Whether one's primary idea is of the estimate he seeks from men, or the estimate he holds of himself, it bars him from the presence of God and nullifies his petition.

"And in praying use not vain repetitions, as the heathen do: for they think that they shall be heard for their much speaking. Be not therefore like unto them." The heathen have a false conception of God, a degraded idea of how to influence him, and a superstitious reliance on ritual half mingled with magic. They use "vain repetitions," such as leaving a lasting impression on any one who has stood and listened in a heathen temple, or even at certain occasions in a Roman or Greek church. For twenty minutes one listened to a group of monks in the Llama Temple of Pekin intone unceasingly: "O, Delai Llama; O, Delai Llama," and it was going on unchecked when time called us to leave. "They think they shall be heard for their much speaking," not knowing that it is eager intensity, not lengthened monotony, that appeals to personal sympathy, whether in God or in good men.

Jesus strongly intimates that these heathen errors may be found in Jewish liturgy and ceremonial, and that they will endanger the praying experience of his own disciples. There is great danger in us all that prayer become formal, a set of ideas largely fixed and of phrases that but slightly vary. All of us can recall the regular prayers of certain prayer-meeting saints, repeated week by week. What is far more to the point, if we will check up upon ourselves, we may discover a powerful tendency to fall into the habit of making our daily prayers, at family altar, or in private devotions, the repetition of an established set of ascriptions, petitions and reflections. Let not non-liturgical Christians deceive ourselves here as to either our public or our private prayers. We are in danger of being just as formal and just as stereotyped as are those who use a liturgy; and with far less dignity and beauty than the liturgies of the prayer books. There is such a thing as a rosary of words that is as formal and ineffective as a Roman rosary of beads or a Buddhist rosary of seeds or precious stones. One can recall preachers whose prayers induced sleep in which one might indulge with security, knowing that at a certain point near the close there would be the click of a well worn

phrase to arouse one in time for the "Amen."
One knows only too well how prayer calls for
honesty in preparation and in presentation and
how often one commits the sin of the hypocrite
and the blunder of the heathen.

Jesus individualizes prayer. When he comes to
the positive counsel he drops the plural "ye" and
addresses each individual soul: "But thou, when
thou prayest." He calls me alone into the presence of God. He bids me withdraw into my
closet—my place of seclusion, "inner closet."
There I am to shut the door. Here there is danger
that I shall deceive myself. It is not mainly a matter of a place of physical segregation. In a measure the synagogue was that. The hypocrite of
Jesus' warning went to the synagogue. I may
have a little prayer chamber in my house that
may be so used as to subject me to all the sins of
the warning of Jesus. If I go at my "prayer hour"
into my "prayer room" and all the household
and the visitors who may call are warned that at
this hour and in this place there is a sacredness
that it is sacrilege to disturb, and if I urge this and
make a show of it, where then is the true privacy,
the honest secrecy, the genuine aloneness with

God? I may be very much aware of the crowd when physically quite alone. On the other hand I may enter my soul's closet, shut the door and be alone with God in any crowd, on the street, in the market place, or in the synagogue. It was this spiritual segregation from the crowd that Jesus sought, this shutting of the soul up with God. Which is not at all to say that it may not be well to have physical privacy also—a place and a time of personal meeting with God alone. Yet, if my proper private prayer can be made only in a private closet in my own house I shall most of the time miss the true meeting with God to which Jesus calls me. If I do not pray in secret I do not pray at all. If I pray in secret I can learn to pray in public.

Jesus tells me that I am to pray in secret to the Father who will reward me. It is to be a transaction between the Father and me, a communion of us two there alone. This in contrast with the crowd, in contrast with public opinion. It is a sad commentary on human nature that the words of Jesus here had added to them by some copyist the word "*openly.*" Thus the text of the Authorized Version came to read "will himself reward thee openly." There was a feeling that the world, after all, must know that God has heard us. He must make it aware that he is on our side. When we have come out of the private prayer God must do something to show to men that we have won his favor. Such is the viciousness of our love of publicity and our pride in religion. No, Jesus did not thus contradict himself. He was teaching us to make prayer a matter of direct converse with our heavenly Father. He has nothing to say about the reward of the Father being "open." That must depend upon the circumstances and must be a matter entirely of indifference to us, when we pray. To have been with the Father in real communion is its own reward. If there are open manifestations of that blessed experience, consequences of the Father's response to us, these will be for his glory, not ours; will help those who see, not exalt us.

Other words Jesus will speak to me as I enter the holy Presence: "Your Father knoweth of what things ye have need before ye petition him." I am not to inform him of my need—least of all to lay before him my desires which may be all wrong or almost sure to be partly wrong. I am to coax

nothing from him. Certainly I am not to over-
come any adverse or withholding will in my
Father while we are there alone. I am not to win
some select favor.

Thus Jesus leads me up to the meeting with
God. No hypocrisy, no self-seeking, no vain repetitions, no heathen misconceptions, no cringing
dread, no informing God what is good for me, no
wheedling. Just an interview with my heavenly
Father. Thus does Jesus bring me to the door of
my prayer closet, bids me enter in and shut the
door. I am left alone with God!

III

THE ATTITUDE

III

THE ATTITUDE

Alone with God! What shall I say? How shall I begin? It is an awful moment. Shut up with God. Not even another human being to share the august experience. It is terrible—glorious, silencing. But I must begin. "Come, my soul, thy suit prepare." Jesus understands—understands as I cannot. He has given me words of address. And that address which he has given me is important, very. For it shows the attitude of my soul in the presence of God. And it is the soul's attitude that counts. The positions or attitudes of the body are very secondary—of no account at all except as the attitude of the body may reveal or effect the attitude of the spirit, of the self. Prostrate on my face, kneeling and bowed, standing, lying upon

45

my bed, sitting in my chair; eyes closed or open, filled with tears or beaming with joy—all this is secondary. There is no merit in an awkward and painful position of the body; surely no value in any position that fixes my mind on my body and its attitude to the neglect of the spiritual position, and of the relation to my God whom I am about to address.

Jesus gives me three words to guide me in this critical moment.

Following the order of the Greek—and this is here the order of spiritual logic, the order of fitness—he tells me to say, *"Father."* By that word of address to God, Jesus revolutionizes the entire conception of prayer. Men never knew until Jesus taught them that God may be approached as Father. Not even the Hebrews learned that most important fact. They glimpsed but never grasped that relation.

Nothing seems to have troubled Jesus more than this failure of men to know God as Father. His longing that they shall thus know him runs through all his teaching. There is no explanation of his presence in human life more central and more fruitful for study than the final sentence in the prayer with which he brings his ministry to a close (Jno. 17): "O righteous Father, the world did not know thee; but I knew thee." He could not remain in his glory and look upon a world that did not know God as Father. It was because no man could come unto the Father except by him that he came to be to men "the way and the truth and the life" (Jno. 14:6). This is likewise the reason that he lays it upon all who come to know the Father through him, as their supreme privilege and duty, to open up that way to the Father for all the world.

Paul finds this fatherhood of God in Christ Jesus one of the most startling and glorious facts in Christian experience. In our redemption we receive "the spirit of adoption, whereby we cry, Abba, Father" (Rom. 8:15). To Gentile-heathen converts, Paul says: "Because ye are sons, God sent forth the spirit of his Son into our hearts, crying, Abba, Father" (Gal. 4:6).

It makes a great difference when one comes to God as one's Father. The relation robs the divine presence of cringing dread; invites confidences, reconciles doubts, inspires faith, begets assurance.

This concept defines the limits of one's prayers. I will ask nothing of my God that I may not expect from a perfect Father with whom are all the treasures of wisdom, righteousness and redemption. I will dare seek all things that such a Father may impart to a child. In his presence I need only to develop and to realize the meaning of that relation. In his presence I shall feel that I must be and must ever seek to become in character and deed all that makes me his son.

Next Jesus suggests that I shall address God as "Our Father"— *Father of us*, in the Greek. Why the *Our?* This plural comes with something of a shock of surprise after the emphasis which he has laid upon the individualism in my approach in prayer to God. He had been speaking in the plural in his general instructions, in all the negative instructions. Then when he came to draw me nigh unto the Presence, he fell into the singular. "Thou, when thou prayest, enter into thy closet and when thou hast shut the door pray unto thy Father who seeth in secret." All this seems to call on me for the most intense, exclusive individualism. He has shut me up all alone there with God. Seemingly all others are to be forgotten. Now immediately I am told that I must take up the plural in my prayer, must say "Our Father"—not "My Father." Here is an arresting thought. What is the meaning?

There in the presence of God I am unable to think of him as having exclusive interest in me. He has a very personal, a very individual interest in me and in my praying to him; in my needs and in my relation to him. With what winning emphasis does Jesus teach us that "Even the very hairs of each head are numbered." I am praying to a Father who is equally Father of all others who come to him. He earnestly desires that every man will come to him even as I am coming. Moreover, while there is a circle of individual affairs between my Father and me his larger concerns with me are such as involve my relations to my fellow men. God is not seeking merely to attach to himself a number of separate souls; he is building a social order. Men do not live in isolation but in society. God could not perfect me apart from my fellows. Hence when I pray to him, when I hold conference with him, it must be as a member of a group, I dare not forget this fact, or the other members of the group. Dr.

Jowett had a great sermon on the words "When ye pray, say *our,*" and he gave to it the subject: "Socialism in Prayer."

My Father misses all his children who come not to his feet in prayer and I must miss them, too; if I really hold converse with him. Some are not there because they do not know him. They have not been told concerning him. The deepest lament of the heart of Jesus was that men did not know his Father as their Father. His heart breaks forth in a cry of anguished longing: "O righteous Father the world did not know thee; but I knew them." This is the explanation of his incarnation. He could not leave men unable to call upon God as Father even at the cost of the humiliation of incarnation and the shame of the crucifixion. Since "no man hath seen God at any time" in his true character, "the only begotten Son, who is in the bosom of the Father, he hath made him manifest."

Sin, with its superstition, ignorance, vice, iniquity, depravity, holds men back from the presence of the Father. "God commendeth his own love toward us in that while we were yet sinners Christ died for us." It is to this God that we pray.

We cannot pray to this God without, in our measure, sharing his transcendent concern for those who "are yet sinners" and do not come to him. When ye pray say "Our." That is an essential factor in the attitude of the praying soul alone with God. I cannot pray to him for anything that will not make me a better member of society.

Let none deceive themselves by seeking to limit the scope of the "our." To be sure this is the prayer of the men of the kingdom of God. But it is to miss the meaning of that kingdom and to fail in sympathy with the heart of the King when we grow exclusive in our thought of it. Men of the kingdom are to let their lights shine before men that they may see the good works of them that know God in Christ Jesus and glorify their Father who is in heaven. If we are not eager for all men to glorify him we are not prepared to pray to him. Nor let us look forward merely to some future "age" for the coming of the nations to worship at his footstool, and so make ourselves content while the millions know not the Father and while his heart waits for their coming. No, when I say "Our Father" I must feel in my soul the loss of the brothers who are absent from the Father, and must have an active longing for them to join with me in the blessedness of converse with him.

This is the prayer of the kingdom of heaven. We cannot think that Jesus means that we shall wait and waste energy in controversy over the question whether none may use the prayer but those who have definitely and formally come into the kingdom. If there are those whose theology would prevent their permitting or encouraging little children to use the words of the Lord's Prayer, surely the Lord would himself reply again: "Suffer the little children to come unto me, and forbid them not: for to such belongeth the kingdom of God" (Lu. 18:15-16).

No man cometh unto the Father but by the Christ. Let that be taught—but taught as a fact and not as a denial; taught as an invitation, not as a warning.

A later word of Jesus authorizes us to unite him with ourselves in coming to God as "Our Father." John reports his resurrection message to his "brethren," sent by Mary (20:17); "I ascend unto my Father and your Father, and my God and your God." Also (Mt. 18:19-20), he tells us that "if two of us shall agree on earth as touching anything that they shall ask, it shall be done for them by this Father who is in heaven. For when two or three are gathered together in his name there is he in the midst of them." In this sense and in this way our prayer to the Father is to the Father of the Lord Jesus Christ who is united with us when we pray in him. Our Father thus becomes the Father of Jesus Christ and me. When he leads me to the secret prayer with "Our Father," he joins with me in the prayer and permits me to join myself with him as I say in behalf of him and me—now united in interest and in relation with God— "Our Father." As I may ask nothing of my Father that is not to the advantage of all his children, so also I may ask for nothing in which Jesus will not join me. My desires in the presence of his Father and mine must be tested and sanctified by that which he also desires.

Say, "Our Father *who art in heaven.*"

God is not limited by space, or in space. Already Jesus has taken me to my closet, and God is there—he and I closeted together. Yet "Heaven is his dwelling place." The phrase stands for the nature of God and his resources. Heaven stands for the perfection of beauty, character, conditions, glory. Here there is another limit to my prayer—a limit that is also a fresh indication of limitless possibilities. If my Father is "in heaven," then I can expect from him only such gifts as can come from heaven, and such as will make me heavenly, fit for heaven. All that comes to me from heaven will make my life and my world more heavenly. In prayer I am making a link between earth and heaven; am opening up a channel for heaven's bounty to come into this world. Jesus says to us: "I have chosen you, that ye should go and bear fruit, and that your fruit should abide: that whatsoever ye shall ask of the Father in my name, he may give it you" (Jno. 14:16). He would have our prayer to the Father to be the experience through which the abiding fruits of heaven shall be made possible "in abundance" in our lives upon earth.

I have not, then, come to prayer to gain divine power for doing worldly tasks, or for realizing worldly ends. I am come to open the way for heaven's ideals, conditions, qualities, purposes, blessings to flow down into the earth. I came not to harness the power of heaven to the machinery of my earthy plans, but to open the door of heaven for godliness to come down. I cannot ask for anything contrary to the character of God, for anything out of keeping with the heavenly order. To the Father of all, who is in heaven, I come with eager, reverent humility; and with full energy of soul I face him in behalf of his interest in us all.

IV

ONE SUPREME OBJECTIVE

IV

ONE SUPREME OBJECTIVE

Now that I have come into this praying attitude to God as "Our Father who art in heaven"; he listens for my petition. What is it that I shall ask for? I came to him with many desires. My needs were great and numerous. Cares and concerns pressed hard upon me; my business, my family, my ambitions, my wrongs, my disappointments. But when I have listened to Jesus and he has brought me to see how I shall approach and address God, I forget many of the things I had meant to plead before God; I am ashamed even to have thought of some of them, although they had seemed at the time to be most desirable. All the things that I may still lay before "Our Father" have taken on new values in this new relation into which I have come with my God.

Now only one thing seems worthy or worth while. This one thing I see to include all things that a child of the heavenly Father may seek or desire. This world out of which I came takes on a wholly different appearance as I look out upon it from my inner closet with the Father. Values and proportions have all changed. I no longer desire the things I most wanted, nor can I think he would give them to me or be pleased for me to ask for them. No, Jesus has taught me that there is one great, all-comprehensive, satisfying, supremely challenging objective for me. This one thing is that which the Father himself desires and I see now that this alone is worthy of me. Jesus puts it before me in three phrases. They are three cries from the depths of the soul for the one great end thought of in three aspects of it.

The most serious evil in my world, out of which I have come to talk to my Father, is that in that world they do not reverence him. All our ills and woes would pass away if only we knew and loved and reverenced God as our infinite Father. But we do not. Our life is full of sacrilege. It is his world. He made it; sustains it; loves it; sets high value on it; seeks to be glorified in it. But we fail to recognize him and his rights. We seek out many inventions and make our plans, build our civilizations, project our governments, arrange our personal and social lives with little if any effort to make these affairs of ours conform to the ideals and desires of our God. Our world is full of sacrilege. We are profane in speech, more profane in thought, for all treating of life and of God's material and forces as if they are merely secular is to profane them. All assertion of ownership and all conduct that finds the end in ourselves and ignores God is profaning that which is holy. We profane the family by ignoring its divine origin and ideal and using it as an instrument to personal advantage or to mere social convenience. We leave God out of the family life when he should be in it all. We profane our culture by overlooking and omitting its religious element and its eternal significance; by making it merely temporal, material, naturalistic. It is of the earth earthy. We lack reverence for human life and fail to see in every man a holy individual because a potential and purposed son of God. It should break our hearts that so many of God's children suffer needlessly, languish and die cruelly, are born, run out the span of their petty lives and die without ever having discovered their high origin and their eternal value. Men ignore and hate and strive and fight and war and devour one another. They envy and abuse and abase and enslave their fellows. All this in God's world, upon God's men and women and little children, and by those who are themselves God's product, and sustained by his grace. Surely the first, greatest, deepest need is that men—I along with the rest—shall come rightly to think of God and truly to live with him in all the relations and activities of life.

My first petition must be: "Hallowed be thy name." That is what I desire above all things else. I desire in my own life that sense of the holiness of my Father-God that will make sacred all my duties, all my relations, all my undertakings. And I long for this sense of the presence, the rights, the love of my Father to be in all men in my world. So my first and unending petition is for the name—the character—of my God to be recognized and responded to among men.

My mind turns, with Jesus, to the thought of what this hallowing of the name of the Father will mean. Jesus has given me one great phrase for it—"the kingdom of God." That is another way of putting this supreme petition: "Thy kingdom come." I desire supremely to see God reigning in my world. He must reign as Father. Hence his rule must be by the willing, the eager, yielding of men to his control. "Seek ye first the kingdom of God and his righteousness" (Mt. 6:33). Such is the ideal of Jesus for every man who has acknowledged him as Lord. All the teaching of Jesus had the kingdom of God as its subject. All his effort was for the bringing in and the development of that kingdom. It was inevitable therefore that this end should be the supreme objective of the prayer he would have all men to make who pray to his Father. If we honor the name of the Father we must supremely desire to see him reigning in all life. The world in which we live and from which we go to our meeting with the heavenly Father has all kinds of organized life. But few of these organizations are under the full and ready rule of God. Its kingdoms are not God's kingdom. In the Revelation the consummation of history, the full outcome of the working together of providence and grace is proclaimed by "great voices in heaven" at the sounding of the trumpet of the seventh angel: "The kingdom of the world is become the kingdom of our Lord, and of his Christ: and he shall reign forever and ever" (11:15).

As in political government so also in economic and commercial organization the life of our world is not constructed with a view to the rule of God. Our entire social structure lacks the idealism, the spirit and the motive of the divine rule. In such prayer as Jesus leads us into we feel that fact grievously and the soul cries out in behalf of all the world for the rule of God.

The instruction of Jesus becomes yet more concrete, more definite, in the third phrase in which he states for us the petition of the great objective: "Thy will be done on earth." Reverence for God awakens in the soul a passion for the ideal of the perfect rule of God in the world and we cannot rest unless we can see that kingdom coming. We catch up the promise in Isaiah 9:7, and we must be able to observe that "of the increase of his government and of peace there shall be no end upon the throne of David, and upon his Kingdom, to establish it and to uphold it with justice and with righteousness, from henceforth and forever." When we see that Jesus Christ has adopted for himself this promise of his Father, and when we have to come in sympathy with him and in love of him, and under his lead, to our prayer place with "Our Father" we agonize in soul that "the zeal of the Jehovah of hosts will perform this."

But here is no mere emotional cry. We cannot content ourselves with a high ideal sighted merely in an hour of high spiritual exaltation in the experience of fellowship with God. It is a very practical world out of which we have come for prayer and to which we shall presently return. We must go back to the conditions that exist there. We must meet them with a new passion that will express itself in devoted effort to make actual the high ideal of the inner closet. We come out from our conference with the Father "hungering and thirsting after righteousness," in ourselves and in our world. Our heart's prayer alone with God is that his will may be fully done on earth; and that is still our active prayer as we take up the contacts of our world again. We pray as we work. It is a prayer that must be the rule of life under all conditions and in all relations.

There must be the far vision and the immediate insight. "On earth" means the whole earth and we must seek to reach it all with the message of God. "On earth" means on this piece of the earth where I live and I must seek to realize God's will here in my own place and my own environment. The prayer has extensive reach, to the ends of the earth; and it has intensive call to all the energies and aspects of my own living.

The standard for this prayer objective is the highest: "as in heaven, so on earth" is God's name to be hallowed, his kingdom to come, his will to be done. Jesus leaves us no room for compromise. There must be no accepted half measures, no willing half good. Our God knows our weakness and our limitations, and he is very patient with us, if we are honest. Remember that the whole teaching of Jesus here starts from the standpoint of demand for honesty with God. "Ye, therefore, shall be perfect as your heavenly Father is perfect" was the sentence with which Jesus had just closed his outline of the kingdom standard for morals and ethics. From this he turned immediately to the passage that we are studying. We have only to reread Matthew 5:17-48 to know how Jesus was thinking of personal attitude, standards and conduct when he told us to pray: "Thy will be done, as in heaven, so on earth."

Here then is a reconstructing standard and test of the matter and the tone of our prayer with reference to all our affairs and all our desires, for ourselves and for all that we pray for. I must frame my desire and order my heart before God to seek his will in all things. For myself I will ask nothing that does not conform to his holiness within me, nothing that does not build up his kingdom within me, nothing that does not the better enable me to do his will in my life. If it is my business, concerning which I pray, the principle applies. Shall I ask for success, for increase in volume and profits? Not primarily. I am in business with him and for him. I realize that the business of the world needs to be conducted in his name, for his glory; that every form of business that ought to be carried on at all may be made a part of the business of the kingdom of God on earth; that his will needs to be done in the nature, volume, method, profits, purpose of every line of proper business activity. My prayer is that I shall know and fulfil God's will in my business.

Am I coming to God concerning my profession? What it shall be, how I shall prepare for it, how conduct it, what get out of it and what seek to put into it—all will be subject to this kingdom ideal.

Do I come to God with reference to my family? I have no right to ask for them anything that is not for the glory of God. I must supremely desire that they shall "enter into the kingdom of God," and that his kingdom shall be within them. My greatest concern, if I have followed Jesus in spirit into my prayer conference with the Father, is that God's will shall be done by them and in them. If I do not know what will produce this holy result I can only lay them before my heavenly Father and trust him. "For your heavenly Father knoweth what things ye have need of before ye ask him." "If I being evil give good gifts unto my children how much more shall the heavenly Father give good gifts unto them that ask him." And here Luke has preserved for us a form of this teaching that fits exactly into the supreme objective of this prayer: "How much more shall the heavenly Father give the Holy Spirit unto them that ask him." The Holy Spirit will bring my spirit into harmony with the holy Father and I will hallow his name in my life.

Is my child sick? Shall I ask my heavenly Father to make him well? Not absolutely. My first thought even for him should be concerned with whether his living will honor God, for if it does not, it were surely better for my child not to live. Better that I give him now into the keeping of my Father than that I hold him to dishonor God and lose his value in God's Kingdom.

It is the same, then, with every interest of mine. I must seek first to relate it to the plan and purpose of the Father who is perfect in wisdom and goodness. All that cannot, or will not, be wrought into the good plan of God must sooner or later be lost. It cannot live because it is unfit and unworthy.

Here is no call to mere submission. It is not a counsel of quietism. It is no inhibition in energy of will and of action. It is just the reverse. The example of Jesus, and all his words when they

are understood are a challenge and encourage-
ment to the most active energy of our wills.
When I pray for God's will to be done on earth as
it is in heaven, if it is at all true praying, I am
putting myself into the course of the infinite
energy of God; am making myself a medium
and expression of that energy. When my will is
harmonized with the will of God his omnipo-
tence becomes active in the sphere of my responsibility and activity. What I do, he is doing. It is
just as Jesus says of himself, "My Father abiding
in me is doing his works"; and again, "If I do not
the works of my Father, believe me not." The true
son of God, even as his only begotten Son, "can
of himself do nothing but what he seeth the
Father doing." But the positive side is even more
emphatic. The halting until the course of the
Father is known is only to prepare for the most
rigorous and confident action: "What things so-
ever he doeth these doeth the Son also, in like
manner" (Jno. 5:19). When we have been in conference with the Father until we have learned his
will we come forth, as Jesus always did, with a
passionate earnestness that declares, "We must
work the works of him that sent me while it is

day, for the night cometh when no man can work" (Jno. 9:4). Here in the intimacy and the soul labor of prayer man becomes a fellowworker with God and becomes wholly committed in will and action to the purposes of God, so that God worketh in him and he in God to the end of willing and doing that which is well-pleasing unto God (Phil. 2:13).

There is abundant room in man for the surrendered will before God. There will always be room for submission. His thoughts must be higher than ours can reach and his ways beyond our comprehending. He is guiding a universe, working time's history into eternity's prefect destiny. Our knowledge is very limited, our wisdom can at best be but finite, and our goodness is so incomplete as to leave us always partly prejudiced. Our Father is from everlasting to everlasting. He must have his "mysteries, grace, ways we cannot tell." Often we must be still and know that he is God. Often, and in relation to many experiences, we must bow the head and heart to say: "It is the Lord, let him do what seemeth to him good." "Our times are in his hand."

Yet the prayer of Jesus is a prayer of action. It is

the prayer of the kingdom that is in the making and that calls for all the energy of believing men, mastered and guided and made irresistible by the energy of God. "Thy will be done" is not the prayer of an onlooker, but the cry of a worker in the midst of the struggle. It is the experience in which one feels the thrill of the eternal purpose grip him to bear him on in the face of unnumbered foes and of forces of evil, desperate and demoniacal.

"As in heaven, so in earth." The perfect will of God is the soul's prayer unto our Father. It is not a call to God to take us to heaven, but to bring heaven through us into the earth. The soul is not asking for escape but for victory, not for rescue but for infinite reenforcement. We pray not to be removed from an atmosphere of profanity, but for such a spirit of reverence as shall still profane speech, awaken wholesome and saving recognition of the presence of God. God's movement in Jesus Christ and in the Christian enterprise is toward and into the midst of the lost, wicked, depraved, rebellious world. The prayer is not that God will bring us into his kingdom, but that his kingdom may come in us and through us. It is the prayer of a man who sees his world from the standpoint of a holy Father who wills holiness and peace for his world. The hallowed name, the righteous rule, the good will of God, these have now taken possession of my being here in the secret place with "our Father who is in heaven." With him I now face again my world and as I look out upon it he asks me what specific request I will make.

V

THE PETITIONS

V

THE PETITIONS

The Father turns to me and asks: "What are your personal requests, my child?" Looking upon earth from the Father's point of vision has so filled me with longing for its redemption, for the Father rightly to have this honor in the world and to get his will done, that I have become an incident. No I am an instrument. I am more; I am an agent of his to seek first his kingdom and his glory. I am even his child, with a common interest with him in all that ought to be done, all that ought to be changed, all that may be realized in this world of which I am a part; the world from which I have come to talk to my Father; to which I must go again now. I can think of myself and my needs now only in relation to the world and to what the Father wishes to do and to get done in it. "I know him that is true, and am in him that is true, even in his Son Jesus Christ. I now know that I am of God and the whole world lieth in the evil one" (1 Jno. 5:19 f.).

All my prayer for myself must be conditioned by that group of facts which make up the all-consuming experience and which consume my soul with zeal for the glory of my Father. But there are needs of mine; and my Father asks that I present my petitions.

There were many things I thought I wanted. I had come with all sorts of requests in my mind. I would ask him for things pertaining to my family, my business, my possessions. This is all gone from me now; and it has all changed in aspect and in relation. I am to go back into my world for a purpose and with a passion that do not require most of these things which once I longed for. I go from the Father only to work for his glory, his kingdom, his will. All I need, then, is to be kept alive and well for my work. I ask only for support. "Father, feed me, while I work." "Give us to-day the bread which belongs to the day." We live and labor in the Father's care, as we live and labor in his fellowship. Hence our times are in his hands. "We live not by bread alone but by every word that proceedeth out of the mouth of God." All we ask is that he will keep us and provide for us what is needful for the task that his wise love provides for us. Our food and our drink are to do the will of him that sends us back from his holy presence into the world which is to be made holy for him.

In the Father's plans this material provision may come in larger proportions; for he may give us much to do, and so much goods to handle in doing it. If so it will still all be his goods to be used for his glory and we shall have no selfish interest in it. He may strip us of all material goods and give us but the food to keep us alive in order that our personality may be the one source of supply for our working. If so we shall be still in need of much spiritual sustenance. Bread of earth or bread of heaven, we ask for what is needed for "the passing day." How intimately does Jesus thus ask us to live in fellowship with our Father! A great soul in a great service can use great supplies of divine energy. How much, that soul does not know. The Father supplies all as the day comes and goes. The believing soul leaves that to him.

Jesus is but describing his own manner of life with his Father in the world. He lifts us into such exalted position that he invites us to pray that we shall live as he lived, be supplied as he was supplied, be sustained as he was sustained. He warns us a little later—in the latter half of chapter 6 that to be seeking things—food, drink, raiment—is to identify ourselves with the heathen, for "after all these things" they seek. Again, he tells us how useless, how futile, it is to make these incidentals of a temporary, fleshly existence the supreme concern. What a man is anxious about is that concerning which he will pray, if he prays at all. It is a good rule never to be anxious about anything about which we cannot freely pray to God. If we know any thing that we may not seek God's help in acquiring and his blessing in holding we should ask him to put out of us the desire for that thing. Jesus seeks to put us at rest in spirit by bringing us into such relation to the Father and to the Father's objective that we feel no need to ask him for more than support for the passing day. As he is with me to-day so will he be with me to-morrow.

"And forgive us our debts, as also we have forgiven our debtors." This second petition goes to the center of all the social needs—all the social evils—of the world in which we live and into which the will of God is to come and rule. The unfulfilled obligations of men to one another, the wrongs inflicted, the rights withheld, these make up "this present evil world." Because of these there are bitterness, hatred, anger, strife, conflicts, warfare, race hatreds, party strife, personal feuds. All the divisive influences and all the broken unities in our life separate us from God.

There is no possibility that God shall have his rights in our world, and that he shall be able to bring his fullness of blessing into our world so long as these debts remain and so long as those who have been wronged cherish bitterness, hatred and resentment. When we stand with God in the inner closet of prayer and look out upon our world with him, all this seems perfectly plain and infinitely important.

What we see also is that the great debt of every man and of every group is our debt to God. We have misused his world and all the materials in it that came within our power. We have neglected, slighted and often repudiated our responsibilities to him in whom we live and move and have our being. We have turned our faces away from his high ideals and scorned his plans for our lives. Worst of all we have mistreated his children—our fellow human beings. We have looked upon them, as a rule, as mere material, forgetting their humanity. We have resisted their claims upon our sympathy and fellowship, we have used some of them as instruments for our own satisfaction and ambitions. Altogether we have made a miserable moral mess of this world arena which God gives us for a home of brothers under his Fatherhood. Now in his presence and with some deep and vital sense of what it means—and may yet mean—to call him our Father, we see that every sin against brotherhood in all human life in the whole of human history is first of all and worst of all a sin against God's Fatherhood. Here is the basal debt, the all comprehending trespass. The soul cries out:

"Against thee, thee only have I sinned and done this evil in thy sight" (Ps. 51:4).

I see, when I look out upon the world with God, that here is the sum of human ills, the source of all evil, the cause of all oppression and all corruption. I have a great conviction and a corresponding longing that the world shall be harmonized and unified. But the evil has a terrible center in me. I am debtor—manifold debtor—to God. I supremely need forgiveness. I cannot pay. I do not measure up. I am so largely responsible in my sphere for the ills that exist there, that I cannot think of going back into that world without first being reconciled to my Father. I am thinking of going into the world to represent him, to do his will as they do it in heaven. First he must forgive me and let me know that I am forgiven. I come to him, and I am a part of that unholy mass which Jesus calls "the world" in contrast with that "kingdom of God" which he seeks to build. I must be able to return to it more truly "of God" than I am "of the world."

With this conviction filling my consciousness and pressing upon my conscience I see in a new light all the debts, conflicts, transgressions of the life of which I am a part. It may well be that I came to God for help to claim and win my rights in the world against such as opposed me and wronged me. Some of my wrongs were real and many of my resentments may be just enough; but getting them arranged and righted will not much further the glory of God's will in my world. My greatest need is not to get my rights from men, but to get myself right with God. And, furthermore, in the light of God and of my relations to him, it is far more important that my fellows shall have no just grievance against me than that I shall get my full dues from them; that my obligations to others shall be met than that their failures toward me shall be punished. In any case I am the center in which and from which I must now work to get God's will done on earth as it is in heaven.

I must be on right terms with God. I cannot be on right terms with him so long as I am willing to contribute to the confusion and the misery of the human race by harboring hatred or cherishing resentment even for a real injury or a serious wrong done me by some poor fellow sinner in God's world. Once a man comes to feel the importance of being in harmony with God—entirely—and of being truly in fellowship with God in relation to a disordered world, he is ready to forgive all that he may himself be forgiven and may approach the world—enemies and all—as a friend of God. "Forgive us our sins; for we ourselves also forgive every one that is indebted to us." Thus Luke (11:4) reports the way Jesus put it at the later statement of this prayer. The phrasing is significant. Our breaches with God are *sins*, men's failures toward us are *debts*. Feeling the deeper guilt that God must forgive in me I can forgive the wrong, however real, that my brother has done me. God's forgiveness must be continuous for me and I will keep no scores in the wrongs that must be forgiven my brother. For when Jesus said: "I say not unto thee, until seven times; but, until seventy times seven," he meant to remove all limits to the spirit of forgiveness in his followers. He followed up his answers with the parable of the two debtors. The one to whom his generous master forgave him the debt of 10,000 talents ($1,000,000.00) refused to forgive a fellowservant who owed him a hundred denaria ($17.00). The upshot was that the master "delivered the unforgiving man to the tormenters, till he should pay all that was due." Then with urgent application of the parable, Jesus adds: "So shall also my heavenly Father do unto you, if ye forgive not every one his brother from your hearts."

That word "from your hearts" is important and significant. It meets the query so often propounded: How can I forgive unless the evil-doer repents and seeks forgiveness? "From the heart" I can—if I let God into my heart—always forgive. I have forgiven and so hold the forgiveness ready while I eagerly and prayerfully seek the attitude in him that will enable me to deliver that forgiveness and make it effective. Nor must I by any means deceive myself by seeking to limit my forgiveness to my own "heart." If it is really in my heart it will find a way to go forth "from the heart." My attitude toward those who sin against me is to be like that of the Father in heaven toward me and toward all other poor sinners.

Jesus had already dealt with this subject in his Sermon (Mt. 5:21-26). You come to offer your gift at the altar "and there rememberest that thy brother hath aught against thee." And if you

have come in the spirit of true worship and honest prayer God's Spirit will remind you if some
brother has a ground of complaint against you.
You have wronged him. You cannot present any
acceptable gift to God until you have righted the
wrong and made peace with the brother. "Leave
there thy gift before the altar, and go thy way,
first be reconciled to thy brother, and then come
and offer thy gift." Do not take the gift away. You
are to have no thought of surrendering or delay-
ing your worship, except so long as to effect such
a relation with the human brother, as will make
possible a right feeling between you and God.
This you will do so promptly and so speedily that
the gift may rest there before the altar while you
effect the reconciliation. Surely God goes with
the man who obeys this counsel and seeks out
the wronged brother. Presently both will stand
before the altar of the common Father and the
three of them will make up a trinity of love and
fellowship. And a new center of power for re-
deeming that which is lost will have been established.

Jesus deals with the other side of the breach
between men in Mark 11:25. It is in conclusion of

the most emphatically stated assurance concerning our potentiality in prayer that the Bible contains, or that Jesus could make. It is so strong that our translators will not follow the Greek text in giving us the English versions. (It was quoted earlier in this book and the typist declined to follow her notes and changed the tense from past to present.) Look at it (11:24): "All things whatsoever ye pray and ask for, believe that ye received them (got them), and they shall be for you." They will have been assigned to you already by the Father. They will be delivered to you at the proper time, in the loving wisdom of the Father. Instantly Jesus adds: "And"—besides your complete faith, another soul attitude is requisite—"and whensoever ye stand praying, forgive, if ye have aught against any one; that your Father which is in heaven may forgive you your trespasses." *"That your Father may—"* Your attitude of soul conditions your Father's attitude toward you. He *may* only when you *will*.

If I have something against a brother I may then and there before God "in my heart" forgive him and go on with my prayer; but if I recall that my brother has something against me I must leave my gift before the altar and first go seek him and make right my wrong. In both cases the way must be clear between me and my brother before it can be clear between me and my Father. This is the one item in all the prayer that Jesus took up for comment and enforcing emphasis when he had finished the prayer (Mt. 6:14 f.). He lays on the emphasis by a dual statement, both positive and negative: "For if ye forgive men their trespasses your heavenly Father will also forgive you. But if ye forgive not men their trespasses neither will your Father forgive your trespasses."

Nor is this teaching arbitrary. It lies in the very nature of our social relation and of the reason for forgiveness. Remember that God is seeking the true society, a perfect social order. He is at the head of it and at the center of it. All men are united in it. Its very existence depends upon right relations and harmonious fellowship. It exists only in the measure that this unity in fraternity is felt and realized. It is impossible for me to be rightly related to God and unrightly related to my brother in a society in which the Father and brother and I are factors. Any breach is a break in the unity of the whole and a sin against him who is the source and supply of the life and harmony of the whole body. God cannot forgive me if I am unforgiving in my relations within the sphere of his rule and of his heart. Nor should he forgive if he could.

Here, then, I test my desire for forgiveness. Do I really wish God to forgive me? Why? My sin is that I am marring God's society with my ill temper, my ill feeling, my selfish nursing of a wrong. Why do I seek forgiveness? Because I fear punishment, and wish to escape it? Because I wish to be on terms of approach to God for help on which I know I am dependent? Because I wish that spiritual excitation and personal joy that come of such relationship? Or have I come to realize how every break in my fellowship with God is grief to him, a privation in me, a corruption of the society which God wills and seeks and which all men need? When the tragic aspects of broken fellowships and of fellowships unachieved and unsought have gripped the soul, then every sin that hinders that social unity of God and men makes the heart cry out for its forgiveness and for the restoration of the unity. Animosities, bitterness, antagonisms, all sins not only disrupt and hinder the unity, the beauty, the righteousness and the glory of life, but make him who indulges them a small, narrow, incomplete and irritating member of God's world. If I have not realized the meaning to myself, to life as a whole and to God, of all anti-social feeling and conduct, I am little. If I have seen this and still retain my antagonisms, I am both little and mean. All that the world means to God calls upon me to follow the counsel of Jesus and cry unto the heavenly Father to forgive my debts and to pray for insight and power of soul to say, "as I also have forgiven my debtors." Thus alone do I really pray for the forgiveness which I so infinitely need.

One other petition Jesus gives us to utter: "Bring us not into temptation, but deliver us from the evil *one*."

The petition seems to assume the leadership of the Father. I plead that this leading may not bring us into temptation. Is that a strange petition? Does it not grow out of the experience of Jesus himself? When in baptism he had sealed his acceptance of his life mission as the Messianic Son of God; and when, while in prayer, he had heard the approving voice of his Father, and the Holy Spirit had come from the opened heaven "to abide upon him," was he not at once "led up of the Spirit into the wilderness to be tempted of the devil" (Mt. 4:1), when "during forty days" "he was tempted of the devil" (Lu. 4:2)? It was an experience terrible beyond our capacity to realize. From such an experience Jesus would save us, unless duty under God's leading should make it necessary to go into it. Our proper attitude toward temptation is to avoid it, shun it. We are to pray that God's leading will not bring us into it. God's leading we must have. With that leading we can go into and through temptation, but we must not seek it. We must pray that it shall not be our lot. Any path that lacks the leading of God is a way of temptation and the taking of it is already a course of sin. What Jesus is seeking to do for us is to establish in us an attitude that instinctively and consistently desires to avoid temptation. One of the worst tendencies of human nature is that of trying ourselves out in the face of temptation. We wish to satisfy curiosity, to feel the conflict, to try our powers of resistance. Here is one of the chief snares of the devil.

The other part of this petition may look in two directions: "Deliver us from the evil one." The personal aspect of the translation is probably correct—it is "the evil one," not merely general, impersonal "evil" from which we need to be delivered. Men who have felt the intensity of that moral struggle, without which no strength of character emerges, have come to feel themselves at grips with more than an abstract principle of evil, more than a mere conflict of best with good, more than just the urge of the spirit against the flesh. They know what it is to fight with diabolical forces under intelligent, malevolent direction to evil ends.

We pray to be delivered from the evils that beset our path all the time and at every turn. There are evil influences, consciously applied to us and inherent in the order in which our life is set. There are evil inheritances and wicked environments. There are evils of limitation, of ignorance, of weakness. In tempting Jesus the devil took advantage of his hunger and physical exhaustion, of his physical feeling in an elevated position; of his consciousness of Sonship, of his longing to do men good. Evil possibilities attach themselves to even our highest aspirations, our holiest tasks, our finest emotions, our deepest experiences. We need always to be saved from the evil into which we might fall and especially from the evil which we might do. "Sin doth so easily beset us"—for the writer in Heb. 12:1 speaks not of some "one besetting sin" but of sin which in multiform variety so easily entraps us and throws us down, even when we run in the Christian race and would win the crown of successful service and the approval of our Lord.

But the word of the prayer looks further and asks our Father to rescue us—such is the strong meaning of the Greek word—from the evil one. He succeeds all too often in entrapping us. How discouraged, how helpless, how shamed we are when we have fallen into evil and into the hands of the evil one. We need one "mighty to save." Jesus has brought us into this prayer relation to the Father who understands and from whose hands no one is able to snatch and hold us. To him we call, "Rescue us from the evil one."

Here then are the three petitions Jesus puts in our hearts. These are our desires for ourselves as we face the Father who is in heaven, who is also

here with each of us in his private closet in the
midst of a needy world. They are very simple
requests: "Feed me, Forgive me, Fend me in the
midst of evil." That is the prayer of one who seeks
only to be used for the glory of God and for the
good of his fellows. He seeks for himself nothing
but that which will enable him and continue him
in doing good according to the will of God.

It was in some deep appreciation of the spirit of
this prayer that early in Christian history there
was appended to this prayer the ascription: "For
thine is the kingdom and the power and the
glory, for ever."

In the personal petitions, even as in the address with which the prayer opens, the plurals
persist: "Give *us* our bread"; "Forgive *us* our
debts"; "Deliver *us* from the evil one." Our position as members of the kingdom of God is not
lost sight of from first to last. The prayer of the
kingdom is a prayer for the social realization of
the holiness of God. How brief the prayer is.
How few the sentences. Yet into them are packed
all the possibilities that heaven holds for earth.
When this prayer is answered heaven and earth
will be united in the continuous realm of God,

his will will be perfectly done by every man, a perfect human race will be perfectly inter-related and related to God. Every man will have all that he needs and will want no more. Evil will be gone, sin eliminated, the evil one will have lost all his power to debauch or to hinder and to harm. There is nothing we "can ask or think" that a pure heart would seek from the "God of all grace" that is not a part of what Jesus has taught us in this prayer. It remains for us to learn to pray it—to pray it in honest and passionate desire, and loving trusting petition, in unceasing purpose, in unceasing practical effort with all the energy of God in each soul. We must learn to say "Our Father who art in heaven."

"Lord teach us to pray."